AWS Organizations
Hierarchical Structure Challenges

Table of Contents

Chapter 1. Introduction

Unraveling the nodes of complexity that entangle operations in AWS Organizations, this Special Report meticulously tackles the subject of Hierarchical Structure Challenges. No matter if you're a seasoned cloud networking professional or an engaged beginner who's just venturing into cloud management, this in-depth analysis aims to guide your ship through the dense fog of hierarchical implications. Peeling back layer upon layer of technical detail, always in a level-headed, straightforward manner, nothing is left in the shadows. From discussing common roadblocks in dealing with hierarchical structures, to offering solutions, this Special Report is a powerhouse of clarity. By embracing this essential guide, discover the key to turning cloudy conundrums into structured simplicity. When it comes to your AWS architecture, never underestimate the value of knowledge and preparedness - a purchase of this report could prove a wise investment indeed.

Chapter 2. Unveiling AWS Organizations: An Introduction

A well-performing AWS architecture is not just a matter of piecing together relevant services; it also involves diligent orchestration and strategical structuring of various resources. The AWS Organizations adds another layer of technical finesse to your cloud operations by providing a way to centrally manage and govern your environment as you increase in scale.

2.1. An Overview of AWS Organizations

AWS Organizations is a cloud service provided by Amazon Web Services that allows us to consolidate multiple AWS accounts, enabling centralized management of policies, providing better control over our resources, and enhancing our cost and budget tracking. It's one service that takes an account-level management approach, all under one organizational unit, making it easier to manage permissions, improve security, and maintain compliance.

With AWS Organizations, you can logically arrange accounts into a tree structure called an organizational unit (OU). This layering allows for clear delegation of responsibilities, enhances policy enforcement, and significantly simplifies account management. Furthermore, AWS Organizations provides a method for integrating other AWS services like AWS CloudTrail and AWS Config for easier monitoring and compliance checks.

2.2. Delving into the Structure

To begin, within an AWS Organizations structure, you have the root, which lies at the top of the organization. The root isn't an account; rather, it's a place where you can attach Service Control Policies (SCPs) that apply across the entire organization.

Under the root, you can create Organizational Units (OUs). OUs are containers for AWS accounts, and it's within these that you tighten the knot on your operations. OUs enable you to group accounts with similar business requirements or roles and help impose policies according to their relative place in the structure.

Within these OUs, you house the AWS accounts. An AWS account represents an ownership boundary and is seen as the most potent isolation mechanism within an AWS environment. It is therefore essential to affix appropriate account-level restrictions and controls.

You can simplify your management by organizing your accounts into OUs and further nest OUs to mirror your company's functional or business structure.

2.3. Service Control Policies (SCPs)

SCPs are a type of policy that can be attached within AWS Organizations to impact permissions. They allow you to restrict, on a granular level, the services and actions that administrators and users can access.

Unlike IAM policies, SCPs do not grant permissions. Instead, they act as a guardrail to filter the permissions that are allowed to flow within the organization. SCPs help to ensure that your users, roles, and even root users only exercise those permissions that their job necessitates.

2.4. Getting Started with AWS Organizations

To get started, first, you choose an AWS account to act as the management account. This account has unique permissions in that it can perform tasks that affect the entire organization and directly affects every other AWS account in the Organization.

Choosing an account as a management account needs careful consideration as it's not a trivial task to change the management account later, and it assumes the billing for all of the member accounts.

From that account, you can create an organization, add OUs under your root, add accounts to your OUs, and apply service control policies at various levels as deemed necessary — a hierarchical structure that allows for granular control.

Though AWS Organizations bring about a plethora of benefits, understanding its intricate mechanism is of paramount importance to navigate through the hierarchical implications that arise from its setup. By doing this, your transition from managing individual accounts to managing your organization becomes smooth, leading to a more robust AWS architecture with much-needed control, security, and governance.

2.5. The Power of Consolidated Billing

One crucial feature offered by AWS Organizations is consolidated billing. In practice, you can consolidate payments from multiple accounts in your organization, which can lead to substantial cost savings. All AWS usage costs are combined, allowing you to reach volume pricing tiers faster.

Furthermore, it ensures a centralized and unified view of AWS costs, making budget tracking and cost optimization exercises much more manageable.

To conclude, the complexity of AWS Organizations is more apparent than real. By unravelling the nodes that entangle its operations, one by one, you can hone your skills and efficiently manage multiple AWS accounts, leverage cost benefits and enhance security. It may seem like a daunting task in the beginning, but once understood, AWS Organizations can become an essential tool in your AWS toolkit.

Chapter 3. Understanding the AWS Hierarchical Structure

To embark on our voyage through the intricacies of AWS Organizations, we set our first landmark as the understanding of its hierarchical structure. AWS Organizations uses this architecture to arrange your AWS accounts, providing policy-based and hierarchical management. But before setting sails, it's vital to get an idea of the course we're charting. So, let's jump right in.

3.1. The Essentials of Hierarchical Structure

In the world of AWS Organizations, everything revolves around the concept of hierarchical structure, which is founded on two types of entities: the `organization` and the `organizational unit` (OU). An organization is a compilation of AWS accounts, while an OU is a group of organizations. Organizational Units can be nested, giving you the flexibility to simulate your business structure. The highest level in this hierarchical structure is called `Root`.

A simple approach to visualise this hierarchy is:

```
Root
 ⎵ OU: Department 1
   ⎵ Account A
   ⎵ Account B
 ⎵ OU: Department 2
   ⎵ Account C
```

In this structure, you could apply policies at the root level, and they would implicitly apply to all AWS accounts under that root. Similarly, policies placed at the OU level would apply to all AWS accounts within that OU.

3.2. The Anatomy of an Organization

An organization is encapsulated by two primary components - a `Master account` and `Member accounts`. The Master account is your ship's helm, where the administration and management of your organization happen. It's also the only account with the ability to create OUs and invite member accounts. Member accounts, on the other hand, are the crew members - parts of your organization that get managed.

When you create an organization, a Master account is automatically appointed - the AWS account used to create the organization. While this Master account holds significant power, it's recommended it be used sparingly to mitigate unintended changes or security risks.

3.3. Working with Organizational Units

Organizational Unit or OU is a way to segment your AWS accounts for more granular control. It is an environment that can encapsulate multiple AWS accounts or even other OUs, providing an ability to mimic your organization's operational structure.

Whenever a new OU is created, it's always a child of another entity (either the Root or another OU). As an AWS Organizations user, you can nest your OUs, helping you emulate your company's layout efficiently and understandably. This capability plays out as a significant advantage when managing policies that need to be imposed on specific parts of the organization.

3.4. Understanding Service Control Policies

Navigating successfully through AWS Organizations is highly dependent on the knowledge of Service Control Policies (SCPs). SCPs are akin to the ship's compass, guiding how AWS services and actions can be used within your organization.

An SCP is a JSON policy that specifies the services and actions that can be delegated to AWS accounts in your organization. They play an instrumental role in dictating what services and functions the users, roles, and even applications within those accounts can utilize.

By attaching SCPs to entities (Root, OU, or specific AWS accounts), you maintain centralized control over the permitted services across your organization, reinforcing security, and ensuring compliance.

3.5. AWS Hierarchical Structure: Clearing the Clouds

Decoding the hierarchical structure of AWS Organizations might appear complex at first glance. Still, with the understanding of underlying components like Organization, OU, Root, Master Account, Member Accounts, and SCPs, the clouds of complexity start dispelling. Understanding these pieces is the first step in navigating through the labyrinth of hierarchical challenges and embracing a structured environment.

In the upcoming sections, we will dive deeper into the practical aspects of setting up, managing, and optimizing AWS Organizations for your business. We will discuss managing multi-account environments, best practices for complex architectures, security implications, and much more.

Remember, navigating through the cloud might seem confusing and intimidating at times, but armed with knowledge, you are capable of steering your organization through any storm that might come your way. So keep learning, keep exploring, and keep mastering the intricate world of AWS Organizations.

Chapter 4. Common Challenges in AWS Formation and Management

As you embark on your journey to unravel the intricacies of AWS Organizations, a key aspect to understand is the common challenges encountered in AWS Formation and Management. Herein, you'll glean insights into these challenges, along with viable solutions to comfortably overcome them.

4.1. Identifying and Defining Requirements

The challenge of AWS formation starts at the very beginning: identifying and defining requirements. It's not uncommon for organizations to struggle with understanding the specific needs of their applications and resources. If you cannot accurately define your requirements, it becomes immensely difficult to design and implement a structure that serves your needs effectively. It is thus absolutely vital to identify the purpose, usage of resources, scalability needs, recovery measures, and the desired performance levels before proceeding with formation.

Understanding the needs of your applications helps set the pathway for structuring your AWS resources effectively. It's about tying together the puzzle pieces so they form a coherent whole.

4.2. Complexity in Design and Implementation

Another challenge rears its head during the design and

implementation phase. AWS Organizations incorporates myriad services and moving parts. Figuring out the role of each of these services and determining how they interact with one another is no easy task, especially if you're hunting for an optimal formation - one that ensures streamlined operations while maintaining cost-effectiveness.

An intertwined web of services, while rich in functionality, can become highly complex if not understood and managed properly. Successfully navigating this complexity is key to creating a performant and maintainable AWS deployment.

4.3. Management of Interdependent Services

The integral operation of AWS Services can be likened to the gears of a clock. Each service runs in tandem, affected by the operation of many others. However, the creation of dependencies can result in complicacies if an issue arises in one service, leading to a potential collapse of the entire chain. Therefore, application dependencies need to be managed adeptly to ensure smoother operations.

4.4. Understanding AWS Pricing and Cost Optimization

The pricing structure of AWS is complex and can be puzzling especially to the less experienced. The multifaceted nature of AWS's pricing based on regions, instances types, storage, data transfer, service levels amongst others makes cost estimation a challenging task.

Furthermore, AWS provides numerous saving plans and cost optimization methods for the users that can be availed to save on your AWS bill. Comprehending these plans and optimizing your resources without compromising performance, requires adept knowledge of the workings of AWS.

4.5. Security and Compliance

Security is always paramount, no matter the organization or industry. The digital era has raised the stakes even higher. AWS provides robust security measures, but the wide array of controls and policies can become difficult to manage.

In addition, the multi-tenant nature of cloud services means shared responsibility between AWS and the customer. Ensuring that your part of the 'Shared Responsibility Model' is covered becomes crucial to standing guard against security breaches.

Adding to it the compliance requirements - organizations need to ensure they meet all necessary regulations and standards such as GDPR, PCI DSS, HIPAA etc. as applicable. Balancing security and compliance with functionality can be a challenging task.

4.6. Navigating the Cloud Learning Curve

For beginners in cloud management, the learning curve for understanding and utilizing AWS services can be steep. Even experienced professionals may find it challenging due to the sheer breadth and depth of the AWS suite of services. Regular updates and introductions of newer services or features can make this a continuous learning process.

While each of these challenges may seem formidable at first, comprehending and conquering them is definitely achievable. The following sections dive deeper into each of these challenges, illuminating how they can be overcome, and guiding your path towards mastering AWS Formation and Management.

(Please add more sub-chapters accordingly based on the scope of the report. Consider discussing above challenges in detail, case studies, best practices, AWS's Capacity Reservations and Resource groups, managing users through AWS IAM, handling disasters and outages, maintenance, automation etc. as part of the full chapter.)

Remember, the path to mastery is through constant learning and improvement. As you continue to learn and grow, the complexities of AWS formation and management become the stepping stones to your triumphs in cloud management.

Chapter 5. Security, Control, and Governance in AWS Organizations

To begin to truly comprehend the scope and potential nuances of Security, Control, and Governance when dealing with AWS Organizations, it is crucial to establish a foundational understanding of its offerings and inherent complexities. Let's start with a straightforward explanation and then delve deeper as we carry on.

Security, Control, and Governance within AWS Organizations provide centralized governance and management across multiple AWS accounts. In this environment, organizations can create policies that apply to all accounts in their organization. The collection of these AWS policies can be seen as the precedent-setting laws of the cloud infrastructure, which allows for control over necessary permissions for your users.

5.1. The Importance of Service Control Policies

Within the AWS Organizations service, a fundamental element is the Service Control Policies (SCPs). SCPs offer granular permissions control over your AWS service, acting as the primary method for administering permission rights across AWS accounts.

To understand the operation of SCPs, consider their function as the gatekeepers, evaluating every AWS request within associated accounts. Their role is pivotal! They rule over your AWS Services' permission rights, granting or denying access as necessary.

Creating, editing, and removing Service Control Policies requires the highest level of precautions due to their effect on account accessibility. As such, AWS makes it impossible for SCPs to be manipulated by regular IAM roles - only the master account, imbued with administrative supremacy, can exercise this responsibility.

Example of an SCP in Asciidoc syntax below:

```
---
{
    "Version": "2012-10-17",
    "Statement": [
        {
            "Effect": "Allow",
            "Action": "ec2:*",
            "Resource": "*"
        }
    ]
}
---
```

The above SCP allows all actions on Amazon EC2 services.

5.2. Strategies to Improve Governance

Good governance deployed across AWS Organizations can take different forms considering the particularities of each business context. That being said, several key aspects should be hewed to the framework. They include but aren't limited to: access control, resource tracking, security audits, monitoring, and automation.

Access Control Human Error: In most data breaches, human error is the causative agent. As such, AWS Organizations bring to the table various automated solutions to mitigate this risk. Identity Federation, for instance, consolidates the control point, helping you manage access effectively while also eradicating the typical human vulnerabilities associated with password management.

Resource Tracking: AWS Config provides a detailed overview of your AWS resources and a historical timeline of changes made. This allows you to audit changes, ensure compliance, and streamline troubleshooting.

Security Audits: AWS provides you with necessary and effective tools like AWS CloudTrail for conducting internal security audits. This tool helps log, continuously monitor, and store account activity related to actions across your AWS infrastructure.

Automation: AWS Organizations allows you to automate account creation, invitations, and removals. This end-to-end automation aids in minimising operational overheads and optimises governance mechanisms, thereby increasing operational efficiency.

5.3. Compliance Assurance through AWS

Assuring compliance in a multi-account AWS environment often poses a range of challenges. To streamline this process, AWS Organizations offers several crucial features, namely Account suspensions, Compliance reporting, and Automated corrective actions.

Account Suspensions: AWS Organizations allows suspending non-compliant accounts immediately. Accounts can be reinstated once compliance has been ensured.

Compliance Reporting: AWS Organizations allows you to create service usage reports across multiple accounts. This facilitates comprehensive monitoring, ensuring every account follows immutable compliance standards.

Automated Corrective Actions: AWS Config enables automatic response to non-compliant resources detected. Such measures include notifying the user, remediating the resources, or even blocking their permissions.

AWS Organizations brings forth an extensive range of features designed to streamline the management of multiple accounts, maximising your control while enhancing the security, compliance, and governance. However, as with every cloud management tool, the key lies in leveraging these features effectively, making educated decisions, and adapting to the specific needs of your organization. By mastering these strategies, you pave your way to turning the cloudy conundrums that once loomed large into a beautifully streamlined vision of cloud governance.

Chapter 6. Optimizing Resource Allocation in Hierarchies

Controlling and optimizing resource allocation within an AWS Organizations structure can be a complex yet rewarding task, with efficiencies, cost savings, and improved system performance among the ultimate objectives.

6.1. Understanding Allocation Principles

Finding the optimal balance within AWS resource allocation demands a clear understanding of the capacity and limitations of each resource. AWS provides several types of resources - EC2 instances, storage on EBS or S3, data transfer, etc., and each of these resources has its limitations. These limitations may pertain to quotas set by AWS or constraints related to your infrastructure.

Also important to consider is the dynamic nature of resource demand, which can vary significantly over time. Even within the same day, the demand on resources can fluctuously change, leading to potential inefficiencies in resource allocation. AWS provides auto-scaling and other dynamic adjustment features to help manage these changes.

6.2. Practical Application of CloudWatch

To respond efficiently to varying demands, you must possess a clear image of what's unfolding in your environment. Herein comes the significance of Amazon CloudWatch. Amazon CloudWatch is a monitoring service that offers data and actionable insights for AWS, hybrid, and on-premises applications and infrastructure resources. With CloudWatch, you can collect and access all your performance and operational data in form of logs and metrics from a single platform.

Gaining insights from CloudWatch can aid in fine-tuning your resource allocation strategies. Various metrics can flag if instances are under or over-utilized, pinpointing where resources can be reassigned for better overall performance. For instance, should CPU utilization for certain EC2 instances consistently fall below 10%, a different instance type or reduced instance count may be more efficient and cost-effective.

6.3. Understanding Cost Optimization

Achieving cost optimization with resource allocation is about choosing the most cost-effective resources that meet your performance requirements. It includes analyzing your current costs, choosing appropriate resources, measuring your effectiveness, and iterating on your findings. AWS provides various tools like AWS Cost Explorer, AWS Budgets, and AWS Trusted Advisor, all of which can aid in understanding the cost aspects of resource allocation.

By understanding the utilization characteristics of the AWS resources, and knowing your priorities, allocation strategies can be developed to allow for cost savings without compromising computational requirements.

6.4. Leveraging Savings Plans and Reserved Instances

Two specific components that merit further investigation are AWS Savings Plans and Reserved Instances. Both allow for significant cost savings in exchange for committing to consistent usage levels. Savings Plans offer flexibility, applying to usage across any AWS region, instance family, size, and OS. Reserved Instances are available for a broader range of AWS services, but are slightly more rigid in their application.

Using these options efficiently requires some upfront knowledge of likely usage patterns, and a decent capacity for forecasting and planning. Guessing wrong can lead to wasted investment or insufficient capacity. However, if used correctly, Savings Plans and Reserved Instances can become pivotal tools for both resource allocation and cost optimization.

6.5. Conclusion

In the end, it's all about the total value - you want to maximize the performance you get out of each dollar spent. AWS provides a wide range of instrumental tools and features that can assist in streamlining the resource allocation, and yes, it can get complicated. But with a solid understanding of your needs and diligent application of monitoring, evaluation, and planning tools, even the most complex AWS Organizations structure can be tamed and optimized for efficiency and cost-effectiveness.

Chapter 7. Navigating Complex Hierarchies: Techniques and Tools

The dynamic and intricate branching of AWS Organizations' hierarchical structures may present a formidable challenge for those new to the platform, or even for more experienced users. Mastery of these structures plays a crucial role in efficient cloud management, optimizing cost, enhancing security, and establishing compliance across your AWS environment.

7.1. Understanding AWS Organizations Hierarchies

At its core, AWS Organizations allows you to consolidate multiple AWS accounts into an organization. The hierarchical structure of this organization offers a robust, versatile way to manage the various interconnected components. At the very top is the root, which encompasses all other entities within the organization, including organizational units (OUs), accounts, and policies. OUs provide a way to categorize or group AWS accounts with similar functionality, security requirements, or resource usage. By attaching policies to different levels of this hierarchy, you can dictate the available services and actions.

Embracing AWS hierarchical operations can streamline management duties – but only if one properly navigates through the dense maze of complexities. Here, the ability to manage multi-account environments with hierarchical techniques proves vital.

7.2. Familiarizing with AWS Management Tools

AWS provides a multitude of tools designed to combat the intricacies of hierarchical operations. Resources like AWS CloudFormation and AWS Config allow for efficient resource provisioning and configuration tracking. AWS Service Catalog enables the creation of approved, standard AWS resource configurations that keep your environment consistent and well-governed.

Command Line Interface (CLI) and Software Development Kits (SDKs) serve as additional helpful tools. IT teams often adopt automation with AWS CloudFormation templates and AWS CLI/SDKs scripts to increase operational efficiency.

7.3. Dealing with Hierarchical Complexity: Best Practice

The road to managing AWS Organizations can often seem rocky and filled with obstacles. However, an informed strategy can easily help navigate this path. It includes understanding the specific needs of your organization, appropriately designing your organization's structure, continuously monitoring and managing your AWS environment, and evolving your strategy as needs change.

7.4. Mitigating Common Challenges

4 Optimize Resource Allocation: AWS Organizations, in conjunction with AWS Cost Explorer and AWS Budgets, can provide detailed insights into your resource consumption, guiding cost optimization strategies.

Though AWS Organizations offers indubitable benefits, it may also pose certain challenges, particularly in the granular control of permissions, collision in naming conventions, and tracking resource usage.

SCP limits can sometimes prove too restrictive, causing operational issues. To address this, consider implementing a more refined, prudent strategy, reserving stricter policies for areas that mandate tight security. Take care to audit these policies frequently.

A shared organizational framework can lead to naming collisions between resources. To resolve this, uphold a consistent resource naming strategy across your organization using AWS Resource Groups.

Tracking resources can become increasingly difficult as your AWS environment grows. Employ AWS Config or AWS CloudTrail to maintain a detailed record of resource configurations and API activity throughout your AWS Organizations.

7.5. Leveraging Third-Party Tools

While AWS provides comprehensive tools to deftly navigate hierarchical structures, third-party applications may sometimes offer additional capabilities catering to specific needs.

For instance, Turbot offers an on-the-go solution with automated governance controls, bridging the gap that may exist with native AWS management tools. Dome9 allows for increased visibility and security governance across your AWS environment. In short, third-party products often serve as strategic facilitators in complementing native AWS tools, leading to a more holistic, well-rounded environment.

7.6. Harnessing the Power of Hierarchies

By converting the labyrinth of quantification into the straightforward path of qualification, harnessing the power of AWS hierarchical structures need not be an enigma. Utilizing native AWS tools, incorporating best practices, routinely auditing your strategies, and leveraging third-party applications will prove instrumental.

Ultimately, efficient navigation of AWS hierarchical structures signifies a streamlined blueprint, not only for multi-account management and governance but also for transformative strides in your cloud journey. This comprehensive analysis strives to light your path clearly, from understanding the hierarchical structure and available tools, through best practices, to addressing common roadblocks and harnessing third-party tools – guiding you towards structured simplicity. The key, as always, lies within your grasp – knowledge, preparedness, and strategic action.

Chapter 8. Decoding AWS Service Control Policies (SCPs)

The purpose of Service Control Policies (SCPs) is to offer central control over the maximum available permissions for all accounts in your organization, thus forming a critical part of the AWS Organizations security structure. When we begin to decode SCPs, it is critical to understand their role, capabilities, and limitations within AWS Organizations.

Let's start with the basics.

8.1. What are AWS Service Control Policies (SCPs)?

In an AWS Organizations setting, SCPs are one type of policy object that you can employ to manage permissions. SCPs offer central control over the maximum available permissions for all accounts in your AWS organization. SCPs enable you to limit, irrespective of what permissions are granted by IAM user policies or resource-based policies if an action is allowed or denied by the policies attached to the entities (users or roles) that are making the requests.

8.2. Understanding the AWS SCP Language

The language of SCP appears to puzzle new users, yet it's actually quite simple once broken down. Central to their functioning is the policy language, `Identity-based policies` and `Resource-based policies`. Both these policy types use JSON policy documents, containing one or more permissions blocks. Each block has an `Effect` (which can either be `Allow` or `Deny`), a `Principal` (Who is making the request), an `Action` (What actions are being taken), and a `Resource` (which resource is being accessed).

8.3. Applying and Combining Service Control Policies

Understanding the application and combination of SCPs is critical in creating effective and secure AWS Organizations. When you bind an SCP to an OU, the policy affects all accounts in the OU. If new accounts are created in or moved into an OU, the SCPs apply automatically. In more complex cases, permissions are calculated by taking the intersection of service control policies from the root or OU level combined with those associated directly to the account.

8.4. Common SCP Use case Examples

Understanding use cases is a sure path to robust comprehension. Let's explore some common scenarios where SCPs come into the scene.

1. Allow List SCP: This is where only certain services are allowed by the SCP, denoted by "Allow" statements for respective AWS services while everything else is denied by default.

2. Deny List SCP: In extensive contrast to the Allow List, a Deny List SCP allows all services except those explicitly denied by the policy.

3. Read-Only SCP: This SCP provides read-only access to users for listed AWS services.

8.5. Challenges with AWS SCPs

As powerful as AWS SCPs are, they come with their own set of challenges. Erratic behaviours can often occur, mainly because the permissions are the "maximum permissions". These maximum permissions intersect with the IAM permissions to achieve the final permission-resultant, leading to common pitfalls.

1. Conflicting Policies: When policies often contradict, resolution is achieved by the rule of most restrictive outcome. This can be challenging when trying to understand what an IAM user can and cannot do.

2. Accidental Service Disruption: A simple mistake in an SCP could disrupt critical services, as a restrictive policy could inadvertently deny access to crucial services required for operation.

8.6. Conclusion

Decoding AWS SCPs can seem intricate, but with the knowledge acquired, it is easy to see how they form the backbone of AWS Organizations' governance capabilities. Understanding how to utilize SCPs will not only help structure the AWS environment but also enhance security. When done correctly, it is the key to maintaining a well-architected and secure framework in the Cloud.

Anticipate challenges, comprehend the dynamics of applying SCPs, and you will be in command of a secure AWS platform. Rest assured, mastery of SCPs is a significant step towards efficient AWS Organizations management.

With this guide, SCPs should no longer be a convoluted part of AWS Organizations, but a simplified structure that offers maximum benefit to your cloud architecture. Manage your AWS computing environment with relative ease, enabling you to focus more on growth and innovation, and less on administering your cloud infrastructure.

Chapter 9. Best Practices: Designing Effective and Scalable AWS Organizations

In the realm of AWS Organizations, creating a coherent, compelling, and scalable organization design necessitates cautious thinking, taking into account multiple factors such as compliance requirements, billing management, agility, and security, among others. This chapter meticulously enumerates various factors, tips, and tricks for curating a powerful and robust AWS organization that not only meets your immediate needs but also scales efficiently with your future growth.

9.1. Initial AWS Organization Design

Start by constructing a basic AWS organization format. Carefully identify and structure multiple AWS accounts depending on functional requirements. For example, separate accounts for development, production, and testing environments ensure minimal collision and superior security.

1. Key Components of Initial Design

Component	Description
Root	The main entity housing other AWS accounts.
Organizational Units (OUs)	Logical groups for different environments.
Service Control Policies (SCPs)	Define accessible services within an OU.

9.2. Creating Effective Hierarchies

To create effective hierarchies, segregate AWS accounts into different OUs based on the functional, operational, or cost-allocation requirements. In general, it's beneficial to include accounts such as Networking (for shared networking resources), Security (for centralized security administration), and Logging (for aggregated logging) in your AWS organizations.

9.3. Implementing Service Control Policies

SCPs provide central control over the maximum available permissions for all accounts in your organization, allowing you to ensure compliant usage of AWS services. Implement restrictive SCPs at higher levels in your Organization Unit (OU) hierarchy and gradually loosen the policies at lower levels.

9.4. Designing for Security

A secure AWS organization places accounts with sensitive data or production environments in OUs separate from development or testing accounts. Centralized security management accounts can provide an additional layer of security.

9.5. Factoring in Cost Allocation

Creating OUs based on costs can provide a granular view of your AWS spends. Implement cost allocation tags and AWS Cost Explorer RI reports to better manage costs.

9.6. Designing for Compliance

For organizations with strict compliance, having isolated accounts for services subject to compliance, such as services that store customer Personal Identifiable Information (PII), can ensure adherence to standards.

9.7. Planning for Scalability

Design your AWS Organizations with scalability in mind. A best practice is federating access with AWS Single Sign-On (SSO), using consolidated billing, and automating account creation.

9.8. Re-evaluating Your Design Periodically

As your AWS usage evolves, so should your Organizations design. Regular audits and tweaks can ensure overall efficiency and optimal resource usage.

9.9. Pitfalls to Avoid

While designing AWS Organizations, avoid common pitfalls, such as unnecessarily complex hierarchies, overly restrictive SCPs, and underutilization of tagging for cost allocation.

9.10. Enhancing Through Tools

Leverage AWS services like CloudFormation StackSets to manage resources across accounts, AWS Config to monitor resource configurations, and AWS SSO to manage user access.

9.11. Conclusion

Effective design of AWS Organizations requires thoughtful segregation of resources, cost and security considerations, and preparation for scalability and compliance needs. Regular review and essential tools can further enhance the overall structure and efficiency.

Remember, your AWS Organization's design should be tailored based on the needs specific to your business. That's how you ensure turning cloudy conundrums into structured simplicity.

Chapter 10. Case Studies: Overcoming AWS Hierarchical Hurdles

AWS is a monumental platform, replete with a range of services and features. While the platform's strength lies in its diversity, the complexity derived from this multitude can be challenging to unravel, especially in the context of hierarchical structure provisions. Comprehending this cryptic mesh, filled with diverse architectural patterns, requires a deep dive into case studies that have overcome these problems.

10.1. Case Study 1: Streamlining Service Control Policies (SCPs)

One instance drawn from a large E-commerce company reveals how they grappled with unwieldy service control policies within their organization. The company's AWS accounts' structure was organized hierarchically, housing about a hundred accounts. As the number of AWS accounts increased, so too did the complexity of their SCPs.

Before redesign, every SCP modification required a meticulous process, involving SCRUM masters, developers, and IT admins. This not only led to delays but increased administrative overhead as well.

The company circumvented this problem by developing an automation solution. This solution handled provisioning and removal of SCPs using automation scripts and AWS Lambda functions. Such an approach minimized the need for manual intervention and dramatically reduced both overhead and error margins.

In essence, it served as a testament to how automation can assist in morphing intricate tasks into simpler ones, thereby improving their AWS organizational structure.

10.2. Case Study 2: Consolidating Unused Subaccounts

Another story involves an organization that faced a unique problem: following the organizational hierarchy, AWS provided multitudes of subaccounts, many of which were left unused due to project cancellations and other reasons. This proliferated cloud resource waste and increased costs.

The organization decided to consolidate and centralize the unused accounts, a measure that was easier said than done. Each unused AWS account had unique resources, configurations, and even histories, which implied the necessity of a robust auditing system before the consolidation process.

After a comprehensive audit, unused accounts were effectively archived, with the necessary configurations and histories stored for future reference if needed. This rationalization process simplified the hierarchy setup, reduced costs, and allowed for an easier overview of resource allocation by centralizing the cloud.

10.3. Case Study 3: Implementing Cross-Account Roles

A cloud-based software service company found itself working with multiple AWS accounts, causing a struggle when providing access to resources across these accounts. The process was not only time-consuming but ran the risk of manual errors which could have severe security implications.

To tackle this, the company implemented AWS cross-account roles.

An STS token was used for temporary security credentials, enabling access across accounts without sharing long-term credentials. Moreover, they developed a ticket-based system to moderate the access, allowing users access to resources only as long as necessary.

Additionally, they included logging mechanisms using AWS CloudTrail to audit the access requests and fulfillment. This practice brought in considerable reduction in errors, ensured enhanced security, and made the management of hierarchical structures relatively straightforward and hassle-free.

These case studies emphasize that tackling AWS hierarchical challenges can be achieved by applying innovative thinking with elements like automation, rationalization, strict auditing, and moderate access systems. Coupled with the power of AWS, such approaches can turn formidable hurdles into rewarding achievements.

Chapter 11. Future Direction: Hierarchical Structures in Cloud Management

With the accelerating migration of business operations to the cloud, hierarchical cloud management is becoming intrinsic to efficient and secure workflows. Owing to the intricacies associated with multi-level management, a proactive approach is indispensable to unlocking optimum performance. This pursuit of supremacy in cloud management initiates a deep dive into trends and technologies. Acquainting oneself with the implications of future directions is a cornerstone of staying ahead of the game.

11.1. Understanding the Dynamics of Hierarchical Structures

The hierarchical structure in cloud management represents a tiered framework wherein the different parts relate to each other through set patterns and rules. While the root forms the pinnacle of governance, it trickles down into organizational units (OUs) and accounts. Each tier is formulated to serve a distinct purpose, stringent in its design yet flexible in its functionality. The root is generally the hub of control, where permissions and root-level policies are configured. OUs serve to group accounts, enabling blanket applications of policies and global management. Lastly, the individual accounts house the resources and act as the core where operations are enacted.

Here it is vital to understand that the rigidity in structure does not confine creativity. The key lies in the correct approach; adaptability to changing workload requirements and understanding the nuances of multi-tier management are paramount.

11.2. Future Direction: Implications and Challenges

Despite the advantages of hierarchical structuring, we encounter many challenges in streamlined cloud management. One of the most significant is enforcing uniform security control and standards across all entities. As the number of accounts proliferates, establishing and maintaining governance becomes strenuous. Thus, efficient permission management and automation emerge as compelling avenues to explore.

Simultaneously, tiered deployments often create a communication blockade. This absence of transparency results in inefficiencies, redundant processes, and a lack of holistic control. Overcoming this hurdle mandates establishing a feedback loop that permeates all levels, fostering a symbiotic co-existence where changing one variable triggers a responsive ladder of actions.

11.3. Novel Advancements Pioneering Future Developments

As a solution to these hurdles, AWS Organizations introduced a variety of advanced mechanisms and features. With a keen eye on security, AWS launched Service Control Policies (SCPs). These flexible and powerful tools allow you to exercise granular control over permissions across all accounts and the root, paving the way for high-grade, comprehensive security.

AWS CloudFormation StackSets is another counterweight to the hurdle of cross-account operations. The feature enables a unified deployment across multiple accounts and regions, ensuring synchronized execution and propagation of changes, allowing for a truly integrated overview.

11.4. The Age of Artificial Intelligence (AI) and Machine Learning (ML)

The next-generation hierarchical structure is seen evolving with the integration of AI and ML. AI-powered applications can continuously monitor operations to ensure compliance, efficiency, and security. They hold substantial potential for driving proactive troubleshooting, stemming issues at an early stage rather than adopting a reactive stance.

Machine Learning, on the other hand, is pushing the boundaries of operational automation. It harnesses patterns and triggers corrective measures, thereby simplifying day-to-day management. Advancements in ML will only strengthen its role in the future of cloud management hierarchies.

11.5. Laying the Groundwork for the Future

In parallel with improvements and nuances in technology, there is a crucial need to train and upgrade the human element. The skillset required to deploy, manage, and troubleshoot multi-tier management systems is also evolving. Future technicians will be required to wear multiple hats: the algorithm builder, the analyst, the securer, and the troubleshooter.

In conclusion, the hierarchical structure's future paints a picture of efficient and focused cloud management. Yet, challenges loom large and demand exacting and evolvable solutions. A thorough understanding of the dynamics, coupled with the readiness to adopt emerging trends, will lead to mastery of cloud management hierarchies. It is a complex landscape - but navigable with the right compass.